The Presence Of Comfort
A Cardinal Story

To the Special Trips Office!

Marcia Zubretsky

Marcia Zubretsky

Compiled by Kathy Nosal

Misula Press

© 2018 Marcia Zubretsky

All rights reserved. No part of this publication may be reproduced, distributed, or transmitted in any form or by any means, including photocopying, recording, or other electronic or mechanical methods, without the prior written permission of the publisher, except in the case of brief quotations embodied in critical reviews and certain other noncommercial uses permitted by copyright law.

Printed in the United States of America
Cover Art: Marcia Zubretsky
Photo Credits: Author's Collection, Unsplash, and Pixabay
Cardinal Pair Plate: Syracuse China

First edition published 2018
10 9 8 7 6 5 4 3 2 1

Zubretsky, Marcia
The Presence of Comfort / Marcia Zubretsky

ISBN-13: 978-1726189279

ISBN-10: 1726189279

Dedication

To my daughters –
Kathy, Karen, Kristen, and family.

Also, for those of you that have a *thing* that you
find has been special for you in your life.
Its very presence brings comfort.
And, for those of you who don't, yet.

Pretty Songbird

*C*ardinals have been a special bird that we have enjoyed seeing and hearing over so many years in our family.

At our Cape Cod house, there was always a bird feeder or two and hummingbird feeders. We also nailed oranges to trees for oriels in the spring.

A stone birdbath in the perennial garden mostly invited the squirrels to jump on it and turn the cover over.

Many days I'd find the cover overturned on the ground, usually over a lovely flower.

 In the winter, the birdhouses my husband Tom made and put around our property attracted bluebirds.

On sunny days they would roost in their houses, enjoying the day and the sun.

The bluebirds were so pretty and a delight to see in the cold of winter, their blue against the white snow.

The Cape cardinals seemed to stay around the area to nest and have young each year.

They liked the rhododendrons along the front of the house. The cover was dense, and they nested there.

They could see what was going on, but we couldn't see them. Their call was always a giveaway to where they were tho'.

Tom and I became attached to these lovely birds. We watched them year round, becoming familiar with their habits and habitat.

Guardian Angel

After Tom died in the winter of 2008, I was alone in our house.

As the afternoons began to darken and shadows crept in, I'd be sitting in my chair in the family room and looking outside.

There would be this striking shot of red sitting on a rhododendron branch.

The cardinal.

This became a late afternoon ritual. I looked for him each day. It was as if Tom was watching over me and knew that this time of day was tough and it was as if he was saying, *"You'll be alright."*

It was comforting and I thought, at the time, I must be losing my mind.

This cardinal appeared at times that were meaningful to me.

One time I was entertaining my cousin and her husband. We were sitting on the deck enjoying morning coffee. A red flash flew over the deck and nestled in a nearby tree and sat there.

Watching.

I said to them, *"Tom just wanted to be a part of the coffee klatch."*

I explained my attachment to this bird, and they nodded as if they understood.

They probably thought. *"Poor thing, she's lost it. She thinks Tom has been reincarnated as a cardinal."*

That first year after Tom had died I recorded 20+sightings. These sightings were significant with what was going on at the time with me.

I'll list a few along with the ones I've mentioned.

The first time I played golf for the season at Captain's Golf Course in Brewster, MA, I was having a particularly hard round. I teed off on the 16th hole and did not have a good drive. Suddenly I heard that familiar birdsong, and looking to my left, up in a large tree was a cardinal.

Tom always said, *"When things are going not so good with the game, refocus, keep the head down and don't try to kill the ball."*

Well, I birdied that hole, got a par on the next, and on the par 5 got a 6.

Only wish the cardinal had appeared sooner.

When family came to visit in June, we'd be on the deck or working in the gardens or clipping bushes. (Tom's job which he enjoyed a great deal)

Whatever we were doing, the cardinal hovered in the backyard.

In the fall of 2008, I sold some stock. This was when the market and economy had bottomed out, and it was a chore which wasn't in my realm of expertise. It made me nervous.

I came home from the broker and sitting in the rhododendrons was -- you guessed it. I thought, *"I hope I did the right thing with those stocks?"*

My rational after seeing my red friend was,

"I did."

In December of 2008 near Christmas, we had a particularly heavy snow, and I was waiting for the fellow who plowed.

Next to the driveway sat my red friend in a tree. He was there for a very long time and didn't fly away.

All I could think of is he's probably thinking,

"Who's going to shovel this driveway?"

Around Christmas, I put a basket at the cemetery and thought it needed something red. I found a cardinal in a store that I felt would be symbolic and also nice with the greens.

Next time I went to the cemetery, after a snowfall with rain, there in the basket was a white cardinal. The color had all washed away.

It was removed and replaced with a sturdier weatherproof bird.

*Red
Friend*

Since that first year of Tom's passing, there have been many more sightings.

When I moved to Linden Ponds and I've been in my garden patch, there has been a cardinal in the tree nearby at times.

Probably jealous of the tomatoes I've been growing since I've been here.

Tom grew them on the Cape, but never had the harvest like I get with just three plants!

On a recent Memorial Day, I was talking with a friend on the walkway between Woodland Crossing and the Harbor Cafe.

A cardinal was sitting on the fence outside the windows.

It made my day.

My daughters have had significant times when a cardinal has appeared. They just know its Dad either watching or just being "around."

By now you must think we're all ready for therapy of sorts.

I believe there are happenings with "things" that we associate with our feelings at the time. The cardinal is that for me.

I was very vulnerable in 2008 after Tom's passing, and the cardinal was my link to him. I still look at the cardinal as a link. It has appeared at so many events that were either important or significant in my present life.

I have a collection of cardinals. Outside my apartment door there is a ledge, and often I will place an arrangement with a ceramic cardinal nestled in it out there.

When I see a cardinal, I'm excited by their brilliant presence. I know they mate for life. That's a good thing.

Maybe you have a "thing" that you find has been special for you in your life.

I won't laugh at you. I'll say,

"That's wonderful, and I hope it is a comforting presence."

Made in the USA
Middletown, DE
08 March 2019